A Biblical

Understanding of

Self-Injury

Julie Ganschow

MABC, Certified Biblical Counselor

A Biblical Understanding of Self-Injury

By Julie Ganschow
MABC, Certified Biblical Counselor

Published by Pure Water Press,
© 2006, 2013

Cover design by Andrea Loy.

The Bible versions chosen for inclusion in this book are not intended as an endorsement of any particular version but rather for ease of reading. For in-depth study, the author recommends a more literal version, such as the New American Standard Bible or English Standard Version.

The clinical information presented in this book was gleaned from medical doctors, psychotherapists, psychologists, and psychiatrists. All "counselee" representations are fictitious and do not represent any one person living or dead or their actual case histories or personal stories.

Printed in the United States of America

Self-Mutilation

(self-injury, self-harm) can be defined as an attempt to intentionally cause harm to one's own body. The injury is usually severe enough to cause tissue damage to some degree, from superficial scarring to permanent major disfigurement including amputation or mangulation.

SELF-INJURY IS ON THE RISE AMONG TEENAGERS.

Forms of self-injury or self-mutilation include but are not limited to:

- Cutting
- Burning
- Hair pulling
- Eyeball pressing
- Biting
- Picking at scabs/interference with healing
- Punching self
- Extreme nail biting
- Bone breaking (hitting self with a hammer, etc.)
- Anorexia or severe dietary restriction

Cutting and burning appear to be the most common forms of self-injury we are seeing among teenagers in our counseling ministry.

SIGNS OF SELF-INJURY:

- Wearing clothes that cover the arms, legs and trunk of the body when it seems inappropriate to do so. The self-injurer wants to hide the scars of their abuse.
- Having a razor blade, knife or lighter handy.
- Numerous "accidents"

CUTTING IS ALWAYS ASSOCIATED WITH A COMPONENT OF A LARGER PROBLEM.

Some associated problems include:

- Drastic food reduction
- Depression/sadness
- Anxiety
- Borderline Personality Disorder[1]
- Appearing to have "low self-esteem"[2]
- Impulsive behavior/poor self-control

[1]Borderline Personality Disorder is a psychological term for behaviors that are biblically considered to be self seeking. People demonstrating these behaviors are totally self-absorbed, dependant on people instead of God, demonstrate a lack of self-control and impulsivity, respond sinfully in anger, indulge the flesh, are feeling-oriented rather than God-oriented and do not have a biblical view of self.

[2]"Low self-esteem" is a psychological term for what the Bible refers to as "pride." The person does think very highly of themselves and uses manipulation to gain the attention they believe they deserve. Their entire focus is on themselves. This is in violation of Scriptures such as Phil. 2: 3, 4; Matthew 22:39.

3

IS THE SELF-INJURER SUICIDAL?

Not usually. The self-injurer is careful about how they injure themselves so they do not require medical intervention. For instance, they will not intentionally cut over a major artery and will not cut too deeply. Typically they do not want to end their lives; they just want to feel better. The suicidal person will intentionally cut an artery or perform a behavior intended to take their life such as hanging, gunshot or overdose of pills.

WHY DO PEOPLE SELF-INJURE?

The teenage years (when self-injurious behaviors commonly begin) can be traumatic times, especially in our culture where teens are presented with decisions and choices they are not mature enough nor equipped to handle.

Our teens have greater pressures than at any time in history. College preparation now begins in the 8th grade for many students as they have to make choices about advanced placement classes. Many high school students work 20 plus hours a week to save for college, in addition to attending classes daily and doing homework for AP classes. Teens are given mixed messages about relationships and sexual orientation. Sexual behaviors are taught in school and promoted in the popular media. In many cases they are pressured to be sexually active long before they are ready emotionally and physically. Our teens are put in situations they are not ready to handle. They deal with broken homes, spending alternate weekends with each parent and the pressure that comes from being in the middle of divorce. These are only the "normal" stresses our children deal with! This does not even cover the extreme cases of sexual abuse by a parent or step parent, drug or alcohol use in the home by parents who encourage their children to join them in these behaviors, out of control siblings that raise tension in the home, same sex unions, sexually transmitted diseases or abortion.

They come to believe that there is little or nothing they can count on, that is stable and unchanging. Who can they talk to besides each other? Who can they really trust?

All this feeds into the world of self-injury. It is a method of dealing with indescribable pain and loneliness. Self-injurers commonly report they feel empty inside, stressed, unable to express their feelings, lonely, not understood by others and fearful of intimate relationships and adult responsibilities. Self-injury is their way to cope with or relieve painful or hard-to-express feelings.

See the following diagram:

4

Cycle of Self-mutilation
Cutting, burning, hair pulling, head banging, eyeball pressing, biting

Traumatic episode, abuse, neglect, etc.

Inability to resolve pain biblically, anger, rage, frustration, guilt, self-hate, self-blame

Self-mutilation (self-injury, self-harm) can be defined as an attempt to intentionally cause harm to one's own body. The injury is usually severe enought to cause tissue damange to some degree – from superficial scarring to permanent major disfigurement such as amputation.

UNBIBLICAL THOUGHTS AND BELIEFS
Unbiblical beliefs about self:
"I am to blame"
"I am too stupid"
"It is all my fault"
"It will never change"
"I deserve..."
"I am bad, eveil, worthless..."
"No one will listen to me"
"I can't cope"
"I can't handle it"
"How could I do this?"
"I am so angry"
"No words can express how I feel"

These thoughts lead the person to self-mutilate

She cuts or self-mutilates believing it:
Puts her in control (pride)
Punishes herself
Expresses anger over pain she has gone through (rebellion against God)
Will help her to "feel" through the numbing pain (denial) of a past experience
Will relieve the pain of anger, sadness, loneliness, shame, guilt
Will make her feel "alive"
Will help her release all the pain inside

Relief is short lived and guilt, shame and fear at your actions are experienced. The realization that the same circumstances and situations are still there leads to a cycle/repetition with the goal being relief.

Self-mutilation brings temporary relief, a sense of regained control, satisfaction, emotional relief, a calm and peaceful feeling afterward.

WHAT CAN I DO TO HELP?

Unfortunately, there is no quick fix or step by step formula to follow.

If there is a relationship problem with parents or boyfriend/girlfriend, siblings or peers, the troublesome aspects of these relationships must be examined and dealt with biblically. You can learn how to do that.

Many teens come to counseling because their parents force them to come. They don't want to be there, and it usually doesn't go well. They don't know the counselor and do not have an established relationship with them. Those who are forced to come usually have no desire to change.

Honestly, parents, the best people to help your child are both of YOU! God didn't give them to you for you to have someone else raise or deal with their problems. He gave them to you to care for, teach, correct, train in righteousness, and even rebuke when necessary.

Learn to be a question asker rather than a statement maker. If you do not believe your teen will honestly share her burdens with you I would encourage you to develop a habit of asking questions.

If you are not sure how to do these things, may I urge you to take the time and learn?

Take advantage of biblically based training that will equip you to help and minister to your child.

I would encourage you to follow biblical principles when dealing with self-injury rather than going the route of psychotherapy and secular counseling. Secular reasoning is contrary to biblical methodology. Self-abusers don't have an illness that can be medically diagnosed; what they do have is a faulty coping mechanism that is truly a sinful habit.

The biblical perspective on self-injury is that it is primarily a heart issue.

Matthew 15:11 (NKJV)

Not what goes into the mouth defiles a man; but what comes out of the mouth, this defiles a man.

Matthew 15:17-20 (NIV)

Don't you see that whatever enters the mouth goes into the stomach and then out of the body? But the things that come out of the mouth come from the heart, and these make a man 'unclean.' For out of the heart come evil thoughts, murder, adultery, sexual immorality, theft, false testimony, slander. These are what make a man 'unclean'....

Luke 6:43 (NIV)

No good tree bears bad fruit, nor does a bad tree bear good fruit. Each tree is recognized by its own fruit. People do not pick figs from thorn bushes, or grapes from briers. The good man brings good things out of the good stored up in his heart, and the evil man brings evil things out of the evil stored up in his heart. For out of the overflow of his heart his mouth speaks.

The Bible reminds us that in order for our behavior to change in a permanent way, there has to be an internal change first. We humans are very good at making behavior changes – we are just not very good at staying changed! A self-injurer can "pledge" to stop cutting or burning themselves and they may be able to control their behavior for a while. These temporary changes are an indication that there has been no true change in the immaterial part (heart) of the person. Without heart change brought about by a renewal of the mind through the Word of God (Romans 12:2), changes will be fleeting. This will bring a sense of hopelessness to the self-injurer as they come to falsely believe nothing can help them.

The Scriptures and the principles we learn from them about how to think, believe and desire things that glorify God and focus on others can and do changes lives permanently.

A self-injurer has an overall focus on self – on their pain, their loss, their feelings, their wants, their desires. These thoughts, beliefs, feelings, emotions, and desires must be examined in light of Scripture. In other words, the root cause for the behavior must be identified for true healing to take place.

QUESTIONS WILL GET TO THE HEART OF THE MATTER

Jeremiah 17:9 (NKJV)
The heart is deceitful above all things, And desperately wicked; Who can know it?

If you do not believe your teen will honestly share their burdens with you, I would encourage you to develop a habit of asking questions and volunteering answers. You want to expose the contents of the heart through your questioning.

Statements harden the heart, but questions prick the conscience.

Ask them questions that don't allow for a "yes," "no" or "grunt" for an answer. Part of the problem with a self-abuser is they are struggling with pain they cannot verbalize. Asking questions causes us to think instead of emote. It gives us the method to place our thoughts, beliefs and desires into words.

You may want to ask questions like these if you suspect your teen is self-abusing:

- How long have you been cutting, burning or hurting yourself in this way?
- What do you use to do this?
- When did this behavior start?
- Do you do this alone or with other people?
- What happened prior to the first time you hurt yourself this way? (Did someone hurt you, abuse you, etc.)
- Do you recall what you are thinking about while you are hurting yourself?
- Will you make the effort to write down your thoughts before you self-abuse the next time?
- Do you know what pain you are trying to relieve?
- Have you tried another method of pain relief?
- How does cutting, burning, etc. help you? (The usual response to this question is, "it makes me feel better," or "then I can feel something.")
- What positive or godly feelings do you get from cutting, burning, etc?
- Do you believe this behavior is helpful overall, taking into account the entire cycle?

Please notice there are no questions about "why" nor mention of feelings. You want to steer your teen away from feeling-oriented living and into faith-based living. You want to get them to think instead of relying on feelings for decision making.

While everything within you will want to order your child to stop this behavior, I do not suggest that as a first step. Since you are trying to open up communication, issuing such an order will do the opposite. Your child will retreat into secret behavior again and close off from your help.

POINT THEM TO CHRIST

What we all need is to "look unto Jesus, the Author and perfecter of our faith." The self-abuser is no exception. The self-abuser carries guilt, shame, failure, anger, and rejection in addition to whatever drove them to begin this behavior.

Remind them that while some of these (like guilt and shame) are a result of their self-abusive actions, they have all been addressed through the sacrifice of Christ on the cross.

Direct the self-abuser to the Psalms for comfort and for direction on repentance and insight on crying out to God in distress.

Psalm 25:16-18 (NKJV)
Turn Yourself to me, and have mercy on me, For I am desolate and afflicted. The troubles of my heart have enlarged; Bring me out of my distresses! Look on my affliction and my pain, and forgive all my sins.

The Psalmist seeks God first and cries out to Him in his misery. He tells God the sorrows of his heart and asks God for help. He also understands that he has sinned against God and confesses his need for forgiveness.

Hebrews 10:22 (NIV)
Let us draw near to God with a sincere heart in full assurance of faith, having our hearts sprinkled to cleanse us from a guilty conscience and having our bodies washed with pure water.

There should be no fear in the heart of a believer to go before the throne of God. Jesus Christ has given us permanent access to God the Father and He stands as our Advocate before Him.

Ephesians 2:18 (NKJV)
For through Him (Christ) we both have access by one Spirit to the Father.
Ephesians 3:12 (NKJV)
(Christ) in whom we have boldness and access with confidence through faith in Him.
Job 16:19-20 (NIV)
Even now my witness is in heaven; my advocate is on high. My intercessor is my friend as my eyes pour out tears to God.
1 John 2:1 (NKJV)
My little children, these things I write to you, so that you may not sin. And if anyone sins, we have an Advocate with the Father, Jesus Christ the righteous.

The Bible is replete with consolation for sorrow and despair. It is a mistake to think or believe that no one understands our world of pain. Jesus was also tempted to sin; He experienced the same troubles and trials in His life that we struggle with today. Jesus experienced the same emotional temptations as the self-abuser experiences.

Hebrews 4:15-16 (NIV)

For we do not have a high priest who is unable to sympathize with our weaknesses, but we have one who has been tempted in every way, just as we are—yet was without sin. Let us then approach the throne of grace with confidence, so that we may receive mercy and find grace to help us in our time of need.

Jesus Christ was:

LONELY-

Mark 14:37 (NKJV)

Then He came and found them sleeping, and said to Peter, "Simon, are you sleeping? Could you not watch one hour?"

TIRED-

Matthew 8:23-24(NASB)

When He got into the boat, His disciples followed Him. And behold, there arose a great storm on the sea, so that the boat was being covered with the waves; but Jesus Himself was asleep.

Matthew 21:17 (NIV)

And He left them and went out of the city to Bethany, where He spent the night.

OVERWORKED-

Mark 1:35-38 (NIV)

Very early in the morning, while it was still dark, Jesus got up, left the house and went off to a solitary place, where he prayed. Simon and his companions went to look for him, and when they found him, they exclaimed: "Everyone is looking for you!" Jesus replied, "Let us go somewhere else—to the nearby villages—so I can preach there also. That is why I have come.

Matthew 4:25 (NASB)

Large crowds followed Him from Galilee and the Decapolis and Jerusalem and Judea and from beyond the Jordan.

Matthew 9:35 (NKJV)

Then Jesus went about all the cities and villages, teaching in their synagogues, preaching the gospel of the kingdom, and healing every sickness and every disease among the people.

Mark 3:20 (NIV)

Then Jesus entered a house, and again a crowd gathered, so that He and His disciples were not even able to eat.

Matthew 26:67 (NASB)

Then they spat in His face and beat Him with their fists; and others slapped Him,

Luke 22:63 (NIV)

The men who were guarding Jesus began mocking and beating Him.

Isaiah 50:6 (NIV)

I offered My back to those who beat Me, My cheeks to those who pulled out My beard; I did not hide My face from mocking and spitting.

IGNORED/DISBELIEVED/ REJECTED-

Mark 6:1-6 (NIV)

Jesus left there and went to His hometown, accompanied by His disciples. When the Sabbath came, He began to teach in the synagogue, and many who heard Him were amazed. "Where did this man get these things?" they asked. "What's this wisdom that has been given Him, that he even does miracles! Isn't this the carpenter? Isn't this Mary's son and the brother of James, Joseph, Judas and Simon? Aren't His sisters here with us?" And they took offense at Him. Jesus said to them, "Only in his hometown, among his relatives and in his own house is a prophet without honor." He could not do any miracles there, except lay His hands on a few sick people and heal them. And He was amazed at their lack of faith. Then Jesus went around teaching from village to village.

Luke 4:28-29 (NASB)

And all the people in the synagogue were filled with rage as they heard these things; and they got up and drove Him out of the city, and led Him to the brow of the hill on which their city had been built, in order to throw Him down the cliff.

Mark 11:27-28 (NASB)

They came again to Jerusalem. And as He was walking in the temple, the chief priests and the scribes and the elders came to Him, and began saying to Him, "By what authority are You doing these things, or who gave You this authority to do these things?"

John 7:5 (NKJV)

For even His brothers did not believe in Him.

John 10:37-39 (NASB)

"If I do not do the works of My Father, do not believe Me; but if I do them, though you do not believe Me, believe the works, so that you may know and understand that the Father is in Me, and I in the Father." Therefore they were seeking again to seize Him, and He eluded their grasp.

SLANDERED-

Matthew 22:15 (NIV)

Then the Pharisees went out and laid plans to trap Him in His words.

Matthew 26:59 (NIV)

The chief priests and the whole Sanhedrin were looking for false evidence against Jesus so that they could put Him to death. But they did not find any, though many false witnesses came forward.

Mark 3:21 (NIV)

When His family heard about this, they went to take charge of Him, for they said, "He is out of his mind."

Mark 14:56 (NIV)

Many testified falsely against Him, but their statements did not agree.

FALSELY ACCUSED-

Matthew 27:13 (NASB)

Then Pilate said to Him, "Do You not hear how many things they testify against You?"

Mark 3:22 (NIV)

And the teachers of the law who came down from Jerusalem said, "He is possessed by Beelzebub! By the prince of demons He is driving out demons."

Mark 14:57 (NIV)

Then some stood up and gave this false testimony against Him.

HURT BY THOSE HE LOVED-

Mark 3:5 (NIV)

He looked around at them in anger and, deeply distressed at their stubborn hearts…

Mark 15:12 (NASB)

Answering again, Pilate said to them, "Then what shall I do with Him whom you call the King of the Jews?" They shouted back,

"Crucify Him!" But Pilate said to them, "Why, what evil has He done?" But they shouted all the more, "Crucify Him!"

BETRAYED-

Matthew 26:3-4 (NKJV)
Then the chief priests, the scribes, and the elders of the people assembled at the palace of the high priest, who was called Caiaphas, and plotted to take Jesus by trickery and kill Him.

Matthew 26:14-15 (NASB)
Then one of the twelve, named Judas Iscariot, went to the chief priests and said, "What are you willing to give me to betray Him to you?" And they weighed out thirty pieces of silver to him.

Matthew 26:48 (NIV)
Now the betrayer had arranged a signal with them: "The one I kiss is the man; arrest him."

ABANDONED-

Matthew 26:56 (NIV)
...Then all the disciples deserted Him and fled.

HATED-

Matthew 21:45-46 (NKJV)
Now when the chief priests and Pharisees heard His parables, they perceived that He was speaking of them. But when they sought to lay hands on Him, they feared the multitudes, because they took Him for a prophet.

Isaiah 53:3 (NASB)
He was despised and forsaken of men, A man of sorrows and acquainted with grief; And like one from whom men hide their face He was despised, and we did not esteem Him.

John 15:18 (NIV)
If the world hates you, keep in mind that it hated me first.

HUNTED-

Luke 19:47 (NKJV)
And He was teaching daily in the temple. But the chief priests, the scribes, and the leaders of the people sought to destroy Him.

John 7:30 (NIV)
At this they tried to seize Him, but no one laid a hand on Him, because His time had not yet come.

John 7:44 (NIV)
Some wanted to seize Him, but no one laid a hand on Him.

DENIED BY ONE OF HIS BEST FRIENDS-
John 13:38 (NASB)
Jesus answered, "Will you lay down your life for Me? Truly, truly, I say to you, a rooster will not crow until you deny Me three times.
Matthew 26:74 (NASB)
Then he began to curse and swear, "I do not know the man!" And immediately a rooster crowed. And Peter remembered the word which Jesus had said, "Before a rooster crows, you will deny Me three times." And he went out and wept bitterly.

HUMILIATED-
Matthew 27:27-31 (NIV)
Then the governor's soldiers took Jesus into the Praetorium and gathered the whole company of soldiers around him. They stripped Him and put a scarlet robe on Him, and then twisted together a crown of thorns and set it on His head. They put a staff in His right hand and knelt in front of Him and mocked Him. "Hail, king of the Jews!" they said. They spit on Him, and took the staff and struck Him on the head again and again. After they had mocked Him, they took off the robe and put His own clothes on Him. Then they led Him away to crucify Him.
John 19:1-3,5 (NASB)
Pilate then took Jesus and scourged Him. And the soldiers twisted together a crown of thorns and put it on His head, and put a purple robe on Him; and they began to come up to Him and say, "Hail, King of the Jews!" and to give Him slaps in the face…. Jesus then came out, wearing the crown of thorns and the purple robe. Pilate said to them, "Behold, the Man!"
Mark 15:20 (NKJV)
And when they had mocked Him, they took the purple off Him, put His own clothes on Him, and led Him out to crucify Him.

AFRAID-
Mark 14:33-36 (NKJV)
And He took Peter, James, and John with Him, and He began to be troubled and deeply distressed. Then He said to them, "My soul is exceedingly sorrowful, even to death. Stay here and watch."

Going a little farther, he fell to the ground and prayed that if possible the hour might pass from him. "Abba, Father," he said, "everything is possible for you. Take this cup from me. Yet not what I will, but what you will."

Luke 22:44 (NASB)

And being in agony He was praying very fervently; and His sweat became like drops of blood, falling down upon the ground.

John 12:27 (NIV)

"Now My heart is troubled, and what shall I say? 'Father, save Me from this hour'? No, it was for this very reason I came to this hour.

Tempted-

Matthew 4:1 (NASB)

Then Jesus was led up by the Spirit into the wilderness to be tempted by the devil.

He experienced grief, loss, and sorrow-

Matthew 9:36 (NKJV)

But when He saw the multitudes, He was moved with compassion for them, because they were weary and scattered, like sheep having no shepherd.

Hungry-

Matthew 21:18 (NASB)

Now in the morning, when He was returning to the city, He became hungry.

Insulted-

Mark 15:29 (NASB)

Those passing by were hurling abuse at Him, wagging their heads, and saying, "Ha! You who are going to destroy the temple and rebuild it in three days, save Yourself, and come down from the cross!" In the same way the chief priests also, along with the scribes, were mocking Him among themselves and saying, "He saved others; He cannot save Himself. "Let this Christ, the King of Israel, now come down from the cross, so that we may see and believe!" Those who were crucified with Him were also insulting Him.

Luke 23:35 (NASB)

And the people stood by, looking on. And even the rulers were sneering at Him, saying, "He saved others; let Him save Himself if this is the Christ of God, His Chosen One."

I want to assure you that Jesus Christ is intimately acquainted with every sorrow and pain we have. This should be an encouragement to the self-abuser! It means "you are not alone."

During His earthly life Jesus was confronted with all manner of sin committed against Him and He did not sin by abusing Himself. This means there is another alternative – a biblical alternative.

RUN TO GOD WITH YOUR PAIN

Psalm 69:29 (NIV)

I am in pain and distress; may your salvation, O God, protect me.

Psalm 38:8 (NIV)

I am feeble and utterly crushed; I groan in anguish of heart.

Jeremiah 4:19 (NIV)

Oh, my anguish, my anguish! I writhe in pain. Oh, the agony of my heart! My heart pounds within me…

The authors of these verses were in great emotional pain, and they went to God with it. You can go to Him as well! God does not turn His own away in their time of need.

Psalm 69:33 (NIV)

The LORD hears the needy and does not despise his captive people.

Psalm 4:3 (NASB)

But know that the LORD has set apart the godly man for Himself; The LORD hears when I call to Him.

Psalm 34:17 (NASB)

The righteous cry, and the LORD hears and delivers them out of all their troubles.

Go to God in prayer and lay down the burdens of your heart to Him in prayer. If you are a believer in Christ, you will be heard. God cares about you and the weight you carry.

16

Confessing your sin to God is to agree with God that what you have done is wrong.

Psalm 38:18 (NASB)
For I confess my iniquity; I am full of anxiety because of my sin.

Psalm 32:5-6 (NASB)
I acknowledged my sin to You, And my iniquity I did not hide; I said, "I will confess my transgressions to the LORD"; And You forgave the guilt of my sin. Therefore, let everyone who is godly pray to You in a time when You may be found.

While God is never glorified when we sin, He is never surprised. He has known about all our sin since before the foundations of the world were set in place. Yet, in spite of our sin, while we were still sinners Christ died for us (Romans 5:8). Doesn't this give you hope? If God did not turn His back on you while you were unredeemed, He most certainly will not turn His back on you as His child.

Romans 8:1 (NASB)
Therefore there is now no condemnation for those who are in Christ Jesus.

Confession is freeing. God already knows the most secret places of your heart; you can hide nothing from Him. We confess for our benefit, not His. We confess because it is cleansing to the soul, it clears the mind, and it exposes the darkness.

HIDING YOUR SIN (OR ATTEMPTING TO) IS REALLY FUTILE.

Psalm 139:8, 11, 12 (NIV)
If I go up to the heavens, you are there; if I make my bed in the depths, you are there...If I say, "Surely the darkness will hide me and the light become night around me," even the darkness will not be dark to you; the night will shine like the day, for darkness is as light to you.

When a person has gone a prolonged period of time without praying, they mistakenly believe God has no desire to hear them, and they may even think they have forgotten how to pray. Here is a prayer that may help you get started again:

> "Dear Father, I confess to You that it has been a while since I came to You in prayer. I know that You have never left me in spite of my sinful departure from prayer, and the things that I have been doing to myself. Lord, I do confess that I have been harming myself by _____ (cutting, burning or other self-injurious behavior). I am sorry for my sin. I thank You for the forgiveness that is mine in Christ Jesus. Please help me to learn how to glorify You by how I live my life. In Jesus Name, Amen."

Prayer will aid you in cleansing your conscience and relieving you from guilt.

BECOME WILLING TO CHANGE
When you are willing to change it means that you intend to change your behavior, and that you are willing to take the spiritual steps that will cause those changes.

OPEN UP TO OTHERS.
Stop keeping secrets. Open your heart to someone you trust or could grow to trust. Tell them what you are thinking, believing and desiring in your heart. Tell your trusted friend or counselor what you fear and how you think abusing yourself is helpful to you. Choose someone who will be honest with you and won't be intimidated by your self abusive behaviors. The ideal person will not be easily manipulated by your emotions. This is a huge step of honesty for you. Taking this step and seeking out a person will confirm that you are serious about repenting from this behavior.

IMMERSE YOURSELF IN SCRIPTURE.
Romans 12:2 (NASB)
And do not be conformed to this world, but be transformed by the renewing of your mind, so that you may prove what the will of God is, that which is good and acceptable and perfect.

Ephesians 4:23 (NASB)
...and that you be renewed in the spirit of your mind...

Colossians 3:2 (NIV)
Set your minds on things above, not on earthly things.

Reading and meditating on the Bible will have a life-changing effect on your thinking and emotions. As you fill your head and heart with God's Word your thinking will begin to be affected. As you apply what you are reading to your life, your actions will change.

God's Word is intended to change you; it is intended to revolutionize your life.

Hebrews 4:12 (NKJV)
For the word of God is living and powerful, and sharper than any two-edged sword, piercing even to the division of soul and spirit, and of joints and marrow, and is a discerner of the thoughts and intents of the heart.

Begin a catalog of verses that address your problems and memorize them one at a time. When you find that you are tempted to go back to your self-injurious behavior begin to "preach truth to yourself," using the verses you know and have written down.

Scripture says that our struggles are not only against flesh and blood, but are spiritual battles as well. For this reason we are told in this same passage to apply the armor of God in these battles (Ephesians 6:10-18).

SAY "NO" TO IDOLATRY.
1 Peter 4:3 (NIV)
For you have spent enough time in the past doing what pagans choose to do—living in debauchery, lust, drunkenness, orgies, carousing and detestable idolatry.

You may not realize it, but when you self-injure you are practicing a form of idolatry.

Anything you are willing to sin to get is revealed as an idol of the heart. If relieving your internal pain is so important to you that you are willing to sin against your body to get relief then you have made "relief" an idol. If feeling better though self-injury is your goal then you have made "feeling better" an idol of your heart. By submitting to your sinful desire to hurt yourself you are in essence saying that relieving your pain is more important than glorifying God by how you live your life.

For some people the knowledge that what they have been practicing is idolatry is enough to make them want to stop. Others have such a habit engrained in their lives that stopping these behaviors is very challenging.

When you deny these sinful idolatrous desires (the lust of the flesh) you are glorifying God.

ACTIVELY PURSUE HEART CHANGE.

Ephesians 4:22-24 (NIV)

You were taught, with regard to your former way of life, to put off your old self, which is being corrupted by its deceitful desires; to be made new in the attitude of your minds; and to put on the new self, created to be like God in true righteousness and holiness.

This is the process of biblical change. Put off the old behavior- stop doing it! You are being ruined by these old behaviors that are a part of who you were before Christ. Your sinful nature has already been put to death, but the flesh remains with us all through our lives. That is the old self spoken of in this passage. Paul tells us to put it off, meaning that we are to make a decision to stop self-injuring. The passage also says that the flesh is being corrupted by its deceitful desires. "Deceitful desires" are lying longings. They are desires of the heart that mislead and trick us into believing they are needs that must be met and filled for us to be happy, fulfilled, and complete. Some other words for "desire" are: wish, want, longing, craving, yearning, need, and covet.

Your _____ (Insert the word from the above list that best describes what you experience) to experience relief from the internal pain allows you to be lied to by your old self.

What you already know is that when you have the desire to injure yourself it comes with the feeling that it will make you feel better – and it does, for a short time. However, soon after come all the same feelings you had before you cut or burned. This is because your flesh is never going to be satisfied! The more you indulge your sinful desires the greater they will become.

As your mind is renewed by the Word of God you will start to understand that these are false promises that lead to further pain, guilt and shame. In reality, they don't help you with the pain after all. You will see that God has another answer to your troubles and it is found by reading, internalizing and obeying His Word.

This is the "put on" of verse 24. You begin to put the new biblical thoughts into action. Instead of stuffing your thoughts you verbalize them. Instead of cutting or burning your arms and legs you decide to cry out to God for help (pray), go for a walk, call a friend, dance, sing, or go for a drive.

HERE IS A SPECIFIC EXERCISE THAT MAY HELP YOU:

Sit down with a pen, paper and your Bible and make three columns on the paper. In column 1 write out what your thoughts, beliefs and desires are at the time you desire to hurt yourself. In the second column write out Bible verses about those thoughts, beliefs and desires. Search carefully for Scriptures that identify your thoughts, beliefs and desires. In column, write out how you can put those scriptures into action. Make a plan to overcome the desire to hurt yourself and then follow it.

In doing these new things you are denying the lust of the flesh and putting on righteousness.

UNDERSTAND YOU ARE "IN PROCESS."

What I mean by this is that you may fail at this in the beginning and maybe for some time after! You most likely have a long standing pattern of handling your problems this way, and while in Christ it is possible for you to overcome these habits, it may take a little time for you to be completely past the urge to revert to self-injury when things so wrong.

I won't tell you that it is good that you relapse, but it does not mean you are hopeless. If you fail and hurt yourself again, be honest with yourself before God, confess it to Him, tell someone you trust, make yourself accountable to that person or your counselor, and most importantly, determine to put the behavior off, renew your mind, and put on the new self (Ephesians 4:22-24).

Realize that the more you put into practice the things you have learned in this booklet, and most importantly from the Word of God, the less likely you will be to lapse into sinful behavior of any kind in handling the problems of life.

Sanctification is a process and none of us will "arrive" until in God's time we get to glory.

1 Thessalonians 4:3-4 (NIV)
It is God's will that you should be sanctified: that you should avoid sexual immorality; that each of you should learn to control his own body in a way that is holy and honorable. (some versions say in sanctification and honor)

I would urge you to begin the process of biblical counseling with the goal of heart change.

Philippians 1:6 (NIV)

...being confident of this, that he who began a good work in you will carry it on to completion until the day of Christ Jesus.

God bless you on your journey.

About the Author

Julie Ganschow has been involved in Biblical Counseling and Discipleship for more than 25 years. She is passionate about the critical need for heart change in a person who desires change in their life.

She is the founder and Director of Reigning Grace Counseling Cen-ter (ACBC and IABC Certified) and operates Biblical Counseling for Women. She has been writing a daily blog on counseling issues women face since 2008.

Her extensive training includes a Master of Arts in Biblical Counseling, and certification with the Association of Certified Biblical Counselors (ACBC), and the International Association of Biblical Counselors (IABC).

Julie is a gifted counselor and teacher and has authored numerous books and materials for biblical counseling and training. She is also a featured contributor in GRIEFSHARE and a frequent retreat and con-ference speaker.

She makes her home in Kansas City, MO. with her wonderful husband Larry.

You can find her blog at bc4women.org and information about her ministries at www.rgcconline.org, and www.biblicalcoun-selingforwomen.org.

NOTES

Made in the USA
Columbia, SC
12 July 2024

38338925R00015